Finding FREE eBooks
For Your Kindle

Table of Contents

Introduction

So you got yourself a new Kindle. Now what? You could spend a small fortune filling your Kindle up with books! There are literally millions of free books available for your Kindle! Amazon alone has over 50,000 free books. The trick is finding them and getting them onto your Kindle. By the time you reach the end of this guide your Kindle should be overflowing with books!

So what kinds of books can I really get for free? And why are they free? Many of the works available are classics that are now in the public domain. You are probably familiar with many of these great works like Huck Finn, Sherlock Holmes, Charles Dickens, the Greek classics, Shakespeare and many more. Personally, I have been busy acquiring and reading all the Tarzan books I grew up with. All for free! Many other books are released for free by small indie authors who just wish to get known. Many of these books are quite good. New books are frequently offered for free by authors and publishers for a limited time to get some momentum going. It is this last category that we are going to focus on first.

One word of warning before we get started. The Internet and even Amazon's Kindle publishing platform has made it easy for anyone to publish almost anything. No longer is there a gatekeeper checking for quality, editing, formatting or content before its made available to you. Many of the sites I will mention in this guide do put out professional material, but online publishing is kind of like the Wild West yet. As a result, you will find lots of books that are total crap and amateurish! If that happens just delete it and find another book. They are free after all. With a little bit of work though you will also find lots of gems.

If you don't already have a Kindle, you might want to go check out the **Kindle family** at Amazon. I have had the Kindle 2 with 3G for a couple of years now and love it! Its great for traveling too. I have a Kindle Fire on my wishlist but haven't sprung for one yet. It has one drawback in my mind. The screen is like any other tablet or computer screen in that its not readable outside. I can comfortably read my Kindle, with its e-paper technology, even at the beach in bright sunlight.

You don't actually need a Kindle to read Kindle books! Surprised? Amazon offers several **free reading apps**. Currently they are available for iPhone, Windows PC, Mac, Blackberry, iPad, Android, Windows Phone 7. They also have the Kindle Cloud Reader where you can read your books right in your web browser. With the advent of the Kindle Fire a lot more books are coming out with color pictures and diagrams. I recently installed Kindle for PC so I can better view the books that don't render so well on my Kindle. I like it even if its not so portable. Here is a screenshot for those who have never used. You might give it a try.

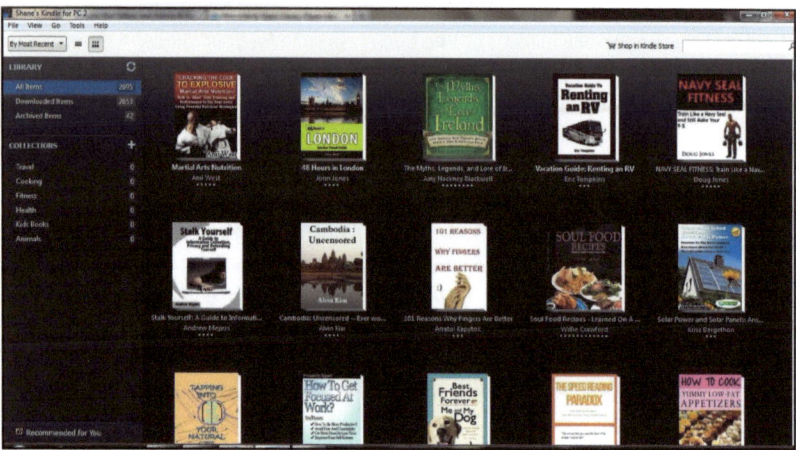

> **Kindle Publishers:** You might want to try a couple of these other methods of viewing Kindle books. Depending on how your readers are viewing your books, they might be seeing them differently that you are. While I do preview my books in Kindle Viewer before publishing, I find that not always way they look elsewhere, including on my own Kindle.

As long as we are looking for free books for our Kindle, let's start with the home of the Kindle – Amazon. Amazon has over 50,000 Kindle books that are totally free! Amazon has a strong interest in providing a healthy selection of free (and cheap) titles in their Kindle store. Free books are a strong selling point. They keep Kindle owners coming back in huge numbers looking for more. And Amazon is well aware of this! What do you do when you go to Amazon? Most likely you were looking for something, and pretty soon you are looking at something else, and before you know it you have bought something! Even I have been guilty of buying a couple of Kindle books after looking through dozens of free ones.

My Favorite Way of Finding Free eBooks on Amazon

Lets start with my favorite method of finding new books as soon as they are free. With the advent of Amazon's KDP Select program many small publishers are making their new books available for free to help promote. The trick is to catch them when they are free. Below I am going to show you an easy way to find several hundred free kindle books everyday.

First go to Amazon and the Kindle Store. Across the top you will see a menu bar looking like this.

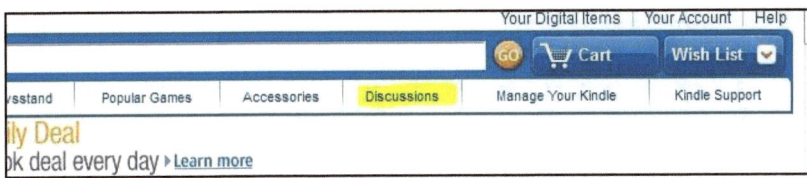

You want to click on **Discussions**. This will take you to the Kindle Forum. Look down the list until you see something saying "Free Books and Chat..." This is what you want. There is also a lot of great info in this forum if you want to browse.

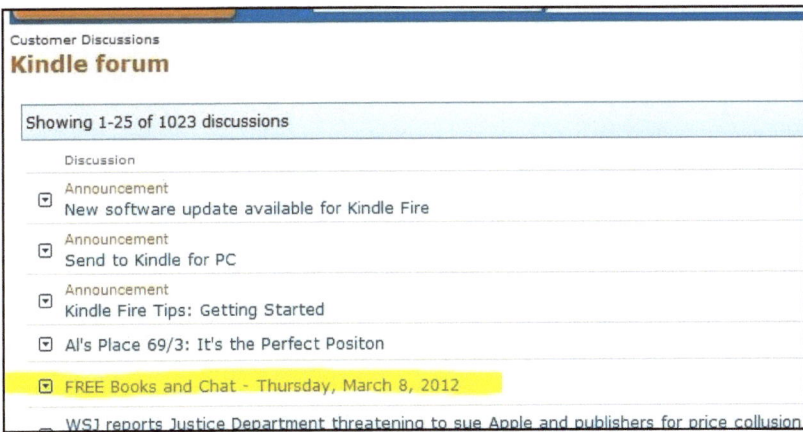

Once there you will find a post looking like this:

I enjoy browsing through everything to see what's new. Usually there will be 1 main Kinlib link with anywhere from 200-400 books on a daily basis. You will sometimes find additional links with a few books that were added later.

UK users – If you look for a thread that looks like this below instead of one above, you will frequently find a links to a UK version also. For some reason UK links aren't usually included in the with chat thread.

Freebie BOOKS - Links Only - Tues, 3/13/12

Charging Kindle in Europe

Can you get a refund for ANY book you buy on Kindle?

Ali's Place 24: Where Two Dozen is Twice as Cheaper

I usually prefer the Kinlib setup, but you might also check out **Ereaderiq**. You will see a lot of overlap in the books listed, but Ereaderiq has a bigger selection. Ereaderiq does give you the ability to sort by category and has more information on their page. Mousing over the book cover will bring up a book description. Ereaderiq also claims to be updated hourly! Ereaderiq is definitely checking out too; and you may find more appealing than Kinlib. The more I explore this site the more I like the way its laid out. Below is a screenshot of a few listings on Ereaderiq.

Note: I use Firefox so keyboard instructions I give will be specific to Firefox; but other browsers should be similar.

All I have to do is highlight the link, right click and click "Open Link" to go right to the page. You should find yourself at a place looking like this:

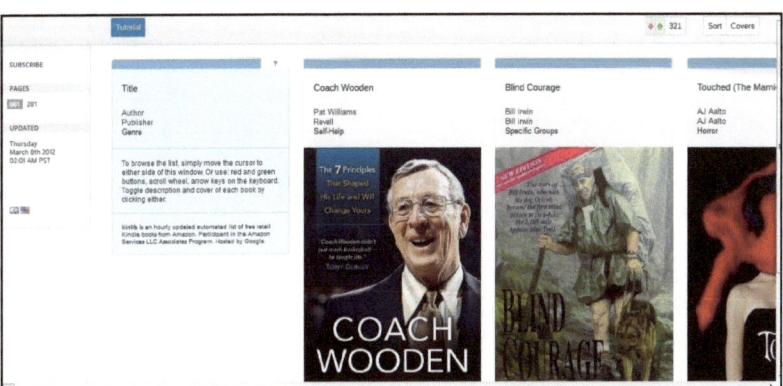

If the page you come to is all text with no cover picture, look up in the top right corner for a button that says **Covers**. Hitting this will toggle back and forth between covers and descriptions. I personally like seeing the covers. Feels more like browsing through a bookstore – something I love to do!

There is a short tutorial there if you need it. Navigating is very easy though. I usually just scroll through until I see something that looks interesting. When you click on a book cover it will switch to a description of that book. Clicking on the book title will take you to Amazon to get that book.

 Note: I prefer to right click on the link and select "Open in New Tab". This keeps my place in KinLib while I go to Amazon to get the book.

I'm just going to pick one that look interesting to show you an example:

Most of us Amazon book buyers should be pretty familiar with this page. Look at the Kindle price to make sure it is in fact free. You should see this:

Every once in a while a book slips in that is only free to Amazon Prime members. If you want the book just hit the **Buy Now with 1-Click** button and its yours! Now you can go back to the KinLib list and look for more great books.

Some things to keep in mind:

- Most of these books are brand new so they may not have any reviews yet. I wouldn't let that bother you. I go usually steer clear of the ones that have a 1 or 2 star rating. If you go down and read the reviews they are usually total crap; poorly written or formatted or even cut and pasted from elsewhere!

- Most of these books will only be free for the day you are looking at them. Don't bookmark them and come back another day because they most likely won't be free.

- If you do come across a book you really enjoyed, please go back and give the book a positive review or a thumbs up. These are what make books successful for the authors. This is also main reason these books are offered for free. So show your appreciation for a good read.

More Ways Of Finding Free Kindle Books On Amazon

One very simple way of finding free books on Amazon is to do a search. For simplicity here is a link taking you to a complete list of free Kindle ebooks as shown below. Notice that there are more than 52,000 books in this list!

> **Kindle Publishers:** This list is sorted by popularity. Did you notice that the top book is a cookbook? Cookbooks can be great money makers on if you know what you are doing. I also find it interesting that the third item is a Kindle game. I've read that tablets are used more to play games on than anything else! Is this also going to be true of the Kindle Fire?

By default the list is sorted by popularity; but you can also sort your list by several other criteria. Take a look at the upper right corner of your search, pull down the menu, pick your option and Amazon does the rest. Most of you are probably already familiar with this but some may not be.

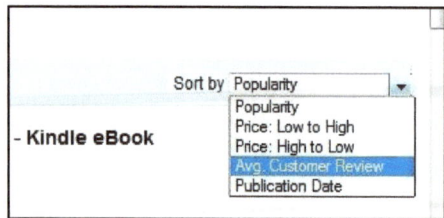

- **Kindle eBook**

> **Kindle Publishers:** Looking at the different results you get from different sorts can give you some valuable information about what customers think are great books, price points, and more. You would do well to study some of the top books to see what they are doing right.

You can also use the menu on the side bar to drill down through the various categories that interest you. I noticed that as you dig this way you start seeing books in the list that are not free or are only free to Amazon Prime Members. So this might have only limited value for digging too far into the categories. That's all right because I'm going to show you another method of digging that will get better results.

Most of us are probably already familiar with the Kindle Best Sellers list. But if you are not here is how to find. You need to be in the Kindle store first. Look down the menu on the left side. You should see **Best Sellers** near the top. Click on that.

This will take you to a page with two columns. The left one is titled **Top 100 Paid**. But if you look to the right you will find what we are looking for – **Top 100 Free**. These 2 columns represent the top books in the Kindle store!

Now if you use the category menu on the menu on the left side you can narrow your search to specific categories. You will still see two Top 100 lists but now they will be for your specific category. And you can keep going deeper and deeper. How cool is that?

> **Kindle Publishers:** This is an excellent way to see what's hot in categories you are thinking about publishing for. See what's popular, what's selling and for how much, what kind of Kindle rank the books have and more.

Are you into the classics? Here are almost 16,000 popular classics offered on Amazon – all free! Just imagine the small fortune you would spend buying all these! This is also a great resource for college students to save on books for their English classes. **Free Classics**

We are just about ready to leave the Amazon site to go explore other sources of free ebooks for you Kindle. But first here are a few more Amazon locations that might be of interest to you:

Pre-Orders: Would you like to see what's coming up in the not yet released section? It's amazing how many books are in this section. I would suspect most of these are from mainstream publishing houses. Note that these are not free books but this list might contain valuable information for a Kindle publisher or a book lover waiting on new books.

Free Games – Kindle Fire (Apps for Android): I'm not into games and don't have a Kindle Fire yet. If I did I would probably be playing games too! Here is a good selection of free games to keep you busy.

Free Collections: I didn't know about this until I recently stumbled upon while browsing. Not only do they link to their classics collection but they also provide several links and instructions to external sites providing free ebooks. Some of these sites I will be covering in more detail. This page is worth checking out though for their instructions on getting the books to your Kindle.

Leaving Amazon Behind

Besides Amazon there are quite a few good sites out there offering free ebooks you can download to your kindle. Most are public domain works, classics, out of print books, and small authors. But there may be better than 3 million free books out there! We are going to start with one of the oldest and perhaps best known site.

Project Gutenberg

These guys have been digitizing books for more than 40 years! They currently have a library of over 38,000 books in ebook format. These are all high quality books professionally done. They offer several formats including epub, kindle, and pdf.

Free Kindle Ebooks: Start here in you search for free books. If you are accessing directly from you Kindle browser you might want to use this link instead: **http://m.gutenberg.org/** Project Gutenberg also has some good advice on recognizing scam sites – those that charge a membership fee to send you to the same books found free elsewhere. Seems there are quite a few of these sites out there too!

From your Kindle you can also download a catalog directly to your device using this link: http://freekindlebooks.org/MagicCatalog/MagicCatalog.mobi where you can easily browse their entire catalog and download book directly to your Kindle.

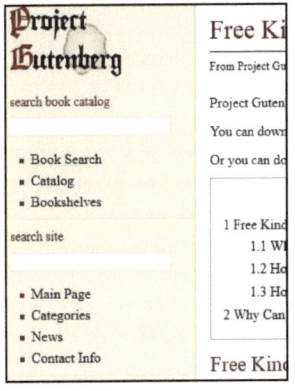

Project Gutenberg is pretty basic and easy to navigate around in. Pick your options from left sidebar.

Book Search will take you to a page with some search options. They also have a couple of quick picks here which might be interesting – Popular, Latest.

Catalog will take you to a more detailed page where you can pick by alphabet, language and more.

Bookshelves is the most interesting to me because this is where they break things down by category. You will have to explore this site on your own to find what most suits you.

Just to quickly show you how easy this is I went to the popular picks and selected A Princes of Mars by Edgar Rice Burroughs. Look at all the different formats available! I'm going to select the Kindle (with images). Many of their books don't have images but they do include them whenever possible.

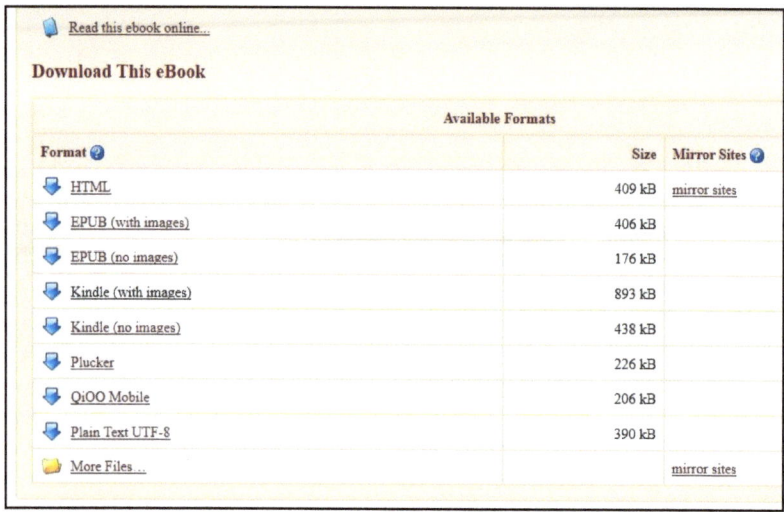

If you have your Kindle plugged in to your computer with a USB cable you should be able to just drag and drop the file to your Kindle. I usually prefer to download to my computer and deal with when I'm all done finding books. These kindle files are in .mobi format.

Something you need to be aware of is copyright info, especially if you live outside the United States. Project Gutenberg says this on their site:

"Our ebooks are free in the United States because their copyright has expired. They may not be free of copyright in other countries. Readers outside of the United States must check the copyright laws of their countries before downloading or redistributing our ebooks. We also have a number of copyrighted titles, for which the copyright holder has given permission for unlimited non-commercial worldwide use."

Open Library

Open Library is an excellent place to find free ebooks, especially if you love the classics! They claim to have over 1 million books available. Their user interface seems to be pretty user friendly and its not too hard to get around the site.

They give you several options to download. If you pick the **Send to Kindle** option they will send you to Amazon to send book through them. Amazon will charge you for this service. I would recommend instead that you grab the .mobi format instead and upload directly to your Kindle from your computer.

MobileRead

You can access this site from the web but it's probably easier to use your Kindle browser to download their guide to your Kindle: http://www.mobileread.com/mobiguide

Once downloaded open the guide up in your Kindle. You will find a clickable list of authors and be able to browse through thousands of public domain titles.

FeedBooks

This site has thousands of public domain books available! Plus they also have a pretty good selection of original books and new authors which are also free. They also have a paid section but this guide is about finding the free stuff.

You can also access this site from your Kindle browser using: http://m.feedbooks.com/

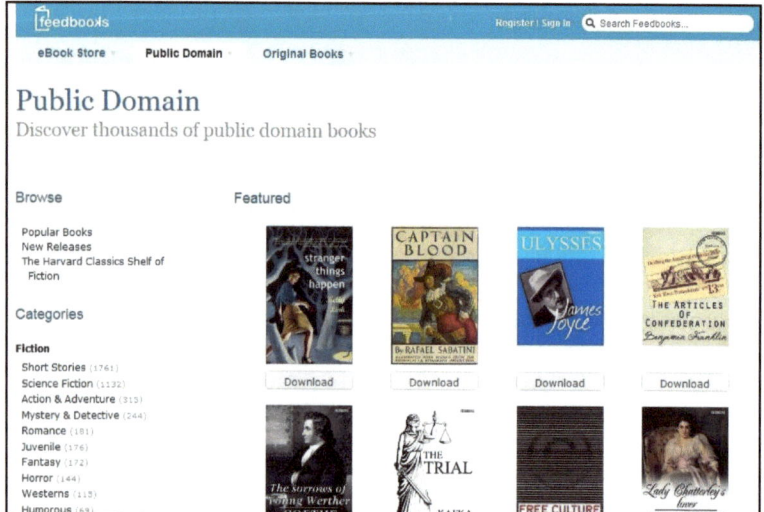

Do not click on the download button. This downloads an .epub document by default which is not supported by Kindle. We will show you how to get around that later. You will want to click on the book image instead. This will access more information about the book and give you available download options.

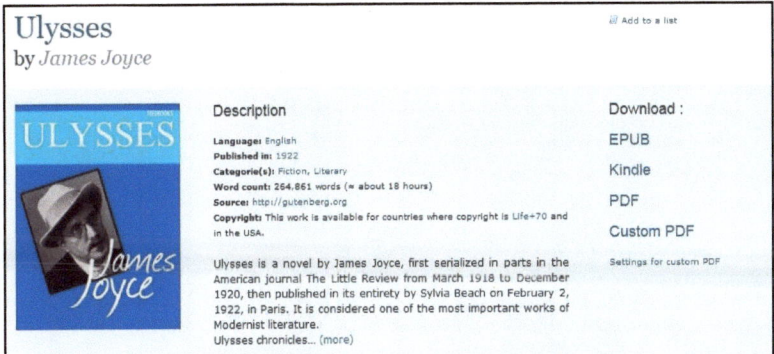

Notice the original source of this book: http://gutenberg.org

---

Kindle Publishers: If you are looking for other places to publish your work besides Kindle, this place will also allow you to publish your books here.

ManyBooks

This site boasts having 29,000 books available and they are all free!

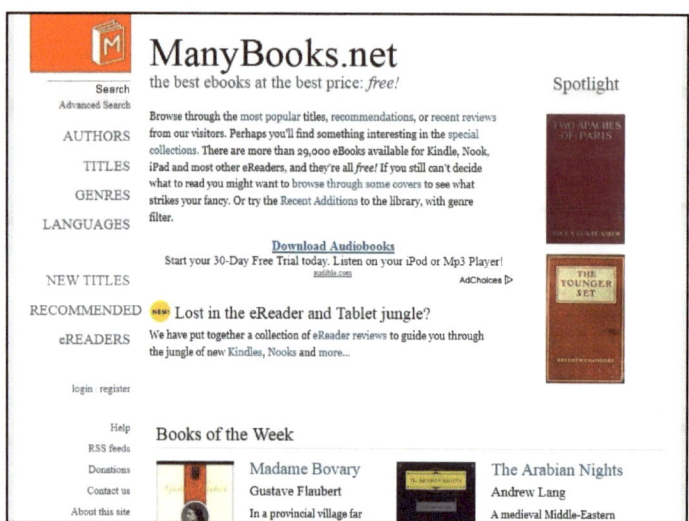

This is a well laid out site that is easy to navigate. They provide excellent books with lots of download options. They even offer the Kindle native format of .azw! I plugged in my Kindle and downloaded Arabian Nights directly in this format. I was bit disappointed in book though. Everything was underlined! Didn't make for easy reading. I will have to try more books from here to see how they turn out.

Google Books Is It's Own World!

Google Books has a huge depository of digital books, including well over a million books in the public domain! There's just one slight problem though for us Kindle users – they're all in .epub format!

Epub format is not a formatted supported by Kindle. I told you earlier though that there was a simple work around to that problem. I'm going so show you how to read all those Google books on your Kindle in a few short steps. Using these simple steps below you will soon have access to the millions of books Google Books has available online.

Step #1

First, lets go to Google Books and find some interesting books. We won't worry about what format they are at the moment. You have a couple modes of finding books on Google Books. The first is the **Advanced Book Search**.

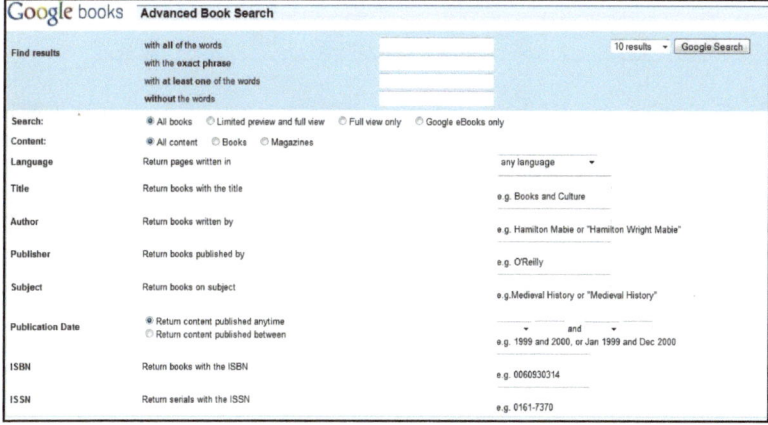

It looks a bit intimidating doesn't it? Its really not bad though. First you want to put at least one search term in the blue bar labeled **Find results**. Then you want to select **Full View** and **Books**. These search criteria will turn up all public domain books plus others that are freely available. Most commercial and copyrighted books will show up as previews only so we want to eliminate from our search. Your search results will look pretty much like a normal Google search. But all the results will have a book image and a few details.

If you aren't looking for anything in particular, you might also wish to try Google Books Browse Mode. This will be a much more familiar interface for you. It is also what I prefer to use unless looking for something specific. Notice that they also have a search box at the top.

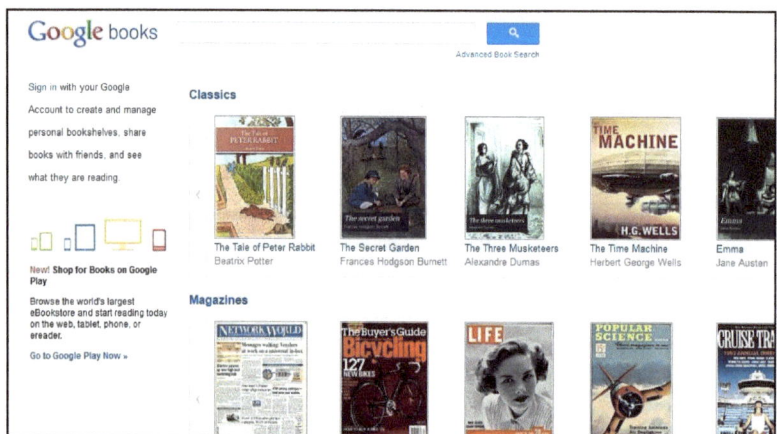

Notice that just mousing over the book covers will give you some information, including whether the ebook is free, preview available only, or available for purchase.

Once you click through on a book you will find a lot more information about the book. The main thing we are interested in right now is how to download our chosen book.

You should see a big red button on upper left that says **Ebook-Free**. Hover your mouse over this and a box will pop up that includes download instructions. For purposes of converting to a Kindle friendly format EPUB is your better choice. PDF doesn't convert as well. But you may wish to have a PDF copy for other purposes. The only thing I don't like about downloading books from here is I get hit with an annoying captcha before each download.

Step #2

Now that we have a copy of our book on our computer it is time to convert it from EPUB format to MOBI format which Kindle happily reads. First, we need to download <u>Calibre</u>, an ebook conversion program. Install the program. During setup it will ask you what your reading device is and will set the output format to that default. I skipped the email setup part as Amazon charges you to deliver your books that way. You may also want to plug in your Kindle via USB cable at this time so Calibre recognizes it. This makes getting your converted books onto your Kindle very easy.

Step #3

Now its time to use Calibre to convert our book. Once you open Calibre you should see something that looks like this:

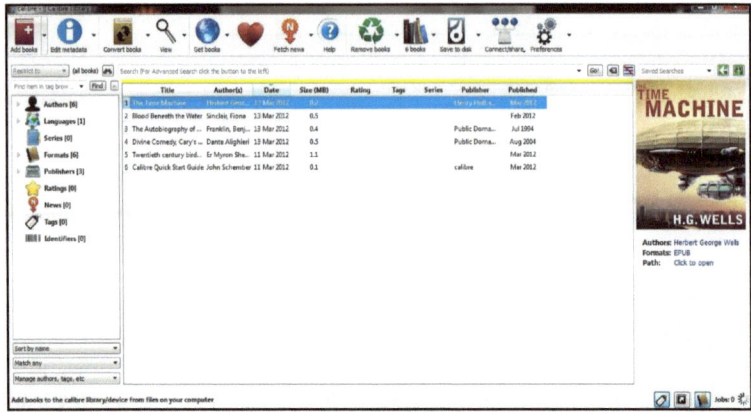

I have already added The Time Machine ebook that I just downloaded in EPUB format. This is as simple as clicking on the **Add Books** button in the top left corner and browsing to find. Now that we have the book in Calibre we are ready to convert it. Make sure the book you wish to convert is highlighted in your list. Now we want to find the **Convert Ebooks** button along the top and click on that. Doing so will bring up something looking like the following.

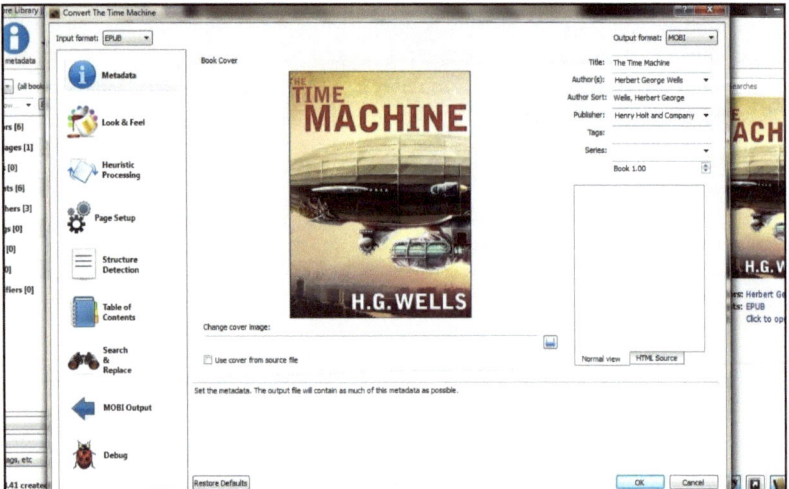

If you wish, you have the option to change the meta data and the look and feel of the output. Double check that it is outputting to your desired format. In this case we want MOBI. If you look down left side you will see an icon that says **MOBI Output**. This is what we want. Looking at the top right you should also see a drop down menu that says MOBI. This is where you can change your output format if need be. There are several formats available. Once satisfied just hit the **OK** button in the bottom right corner. It only takes a few seconds to convert.

Step #4

Now all we have to do is get the book to our Kindle so we can read it. If you have your Kindle plugged into your computer via USB cable, you should see something like below. If not, plug your Kindle in now.

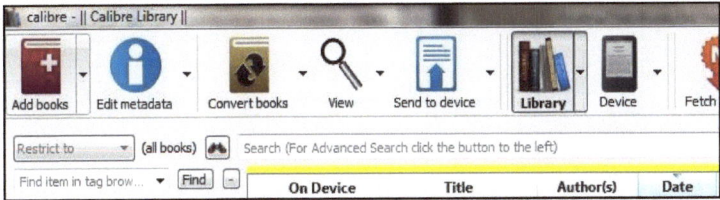

Look for the **Send to device** button. Simply click this button and you book will be on your Kindle. That's all there is to it! When you are ready to disconnect your Kindle from your computer look for the down arrow beside the **Send to device** button. Clicking this will drop down a menu where you want to select **Eject device**. This way you can safely unplug from your computer.

I haven't played around with Calibre much yet, but it appears to be a pretty powerful program with lots of features. You may wish to explore this program further. You can access an online users manual here: http://manual.calibre-ebook.com/

> **Kindle Publishers:** I don't normally enable DRM when publishing my books, but after playing around with Calibre a bit, I will be in the future. Just as a test I grabbed a few books out of my Kindle library in their native .azw format and used Calibre to convert them to PDF, RTF, and TXT formats. In all cases they successfully did so! While this may have legitimate uses where a book owner wishes to print something out, it could also leave you vulnerable to plagiarism by unscrupulous users. Be warned!

More Free eBook Sites

I tried to cover several ways to find free ebooks and several good places to find them. There are lots of good sites out there that I didn't have time to explore in detail. If your quest for free ebooks is insatiable, I have listed a few more worthwhile sites for you to browse below. These are not in any particular order – I just added to the list as I came across more sites.

http://www.diesel-ebooks.com/gbooks/Free-eBooks/results/1.html
http://www.readprint.com/
http://www.baenebooks.com/c-1-free-library.aspx (sci-fi)
http://www.free-ebooks.net/
http://www.archive.org/index.php (over 3 million documents online!)
http://www.justfreebooks.info/ (search engine)
http://wiki.creativecommons.org/Books
http://www.digitalbookindex.com/about.htm
http://www.archive.org/details/texts
http://librivox.org/ (free public domain audiobooks)
http://www.mobipocket.com/freebooks/default.aspx
http://freekindlebooks.org/
http://digital.library.upenn.edu/books/
http://www.podiobooks.com/ (free audiobooks)
http://www.munseys.com/
http://www.freebookspot.es/
http://www.smashwords.com/books/category/1/newest/0/free/any
http://girlebooks.com/ (female writers)
http://www.getfreeebooks.com/
http://www.bookyards.com/
http://www.thefreelibrary.com/
http://www.jungle-search.com/US/kindle.php#free (search engine)
http://www.jasminejade.com/c-115-free-read-ec.aspx (romance)
http://www.fictionwise.com/ebooks/freebooks.htm
http://www.freecomputerbooks.com/

There are lots of free ebooks sites out there. You can always find more by searching in Google for "free ebooks." This is a good way to find some of the smaller sites that are in more specialized niches like computers, gardening, etc. Just watch out for scam sites. If a site asks for money or a credit card to show you free ebooks move on to another site.

Kindle Lending Libraries

The concept of lending Kindle ebooks is fairly new. But a few sites are popping up that allow you to do just that! Now you might be able to just borrow that bestseller you have been dying to read without shelling out your hard earned cash for it. I haven't had time to dig into these sites yet but here are a couple you might wish to check out.

http://ebookfling.com/
http://lendle.me/
http://www.booklending.com/

Amazon also has its own Kindle owner's lending library, but you have to be a member of their **Amazon Prime** program to take advantage of it. Membership allows you to borrow 1 book a month absolutely free! This program is worth checking out for all its great benefits.

Some Thoughts For Kindle Publishers

The Kindle publishing platform is the greatest thing to come along since sliced bread! Never before has there been such an opportunity for anyone to be published. For the average person looking to make some extra money online it is also probably one of the easiest routes to go. You just have to produce quality work, Amazon takes care of all the heavy lifting when it comes to marketing and selling your work. I too jumped into the Kindle publishing game awhile back. I only have a handful of titles up but they are making me a few dollars, more so than anything else I have ever tried online.

In this section, I just wanted to share my thoughts, both from my observations and my personal experience, on Kindle publishing. I'm not a guru or anything but I have learned a lot over the past year or so. I have also learned a lot just by going through the new books on kinlib every morning. I highly recommend for any publisher who wants to see what's going on. I have also bought almost every Kindle publishing product put out. Its appalling some of the total crap has been put forth by some of these guys. And I watched some of it actually end up on Amazon and get slammed by customers. Does anybody actually think you can put out a quality product in 30 minutes or plagiarize a handful of recipes off a website and make something worth spending money on? Amazon customers don't think so!

I might be a Kindle publisher, but I am first and foremost a reader. I have been an avid reader all my life. I love books! And I think you have to approach your publishing this way too if you are going to put out quality products. Look at your product. Is it something you would be happy purchasing as a customer? Or would you be disappointed you spent money on? Or maybe you even feel ripped off because its total crap? Put the customer experience first and you will have a quality product you can be proud to put your name on.

Book Covers

Like it or not people do judge a book by its cover. If that cover is boring or looks like crap they are on to the next book. This is one reason I like browsing through kinlib for new books so much – I get a good look at the covers. Some mornings I will just skim through the selections based on the covers.

Your book needs a cover. It doesn't have to be perfect but it must contain the basic elements a book buyer is used to seeing on a book cover. Believe it or not I still run across books being put up with no cover! Why waste your time publishing if you are too lazy to even put up a cover?

I've read more than one guide by so called gurus who advocate large yellow text on a black background, slapping up a picture with no text, and other goofy ideas. People even put up the 3D covers that came with their resale rights book! Amazon is a flat cover world. Book buying customers have been conditioned to look for flat, professionally done book covers. Anything else just stands out as amateurish or a marketing gimmick and they pass them up.

Can anyone tell me what these books are about?

Neither can I!!!

How do these covers look to you?

We already mentioned first two. The third stands out but they could have done lot more to spruce it up – it looks like a term paper. You can't see it but the fourth does have title on it but its unreadable. Book titles should tell you what book is about. What exactly is *freakout* first aid and what does it have to do with the cover picture? The last one is a travel book. The cover is drab. It could use some bold color and a travel picture.

Determining good or bad covers is sometimes a subjective thing. Here are a few that caught my eye.

The first one clearly tells you what the book is about in both the title and the subtitle. It is also clearly part of a series. The second one is a travel book that is patterned after some of the big publishers with its bright cover and travel pictures. The third book just jumps out and grabs you! And the fourth book? That one is making me hungry! The fifth one just grabbed my attention. If you want some to see some books that are attention grabbers you need to check out the Erotica section. No, I'm not going to show them here! There are quite a smattering of them in the free books. Seems all it takes to grab a guy's attention is a hot babe wearing little or nothing on the front cover! ☺

Copy/Paste and PLR Books

Cookbooks can be moneymakers if you do them right. But there is a lot more to them than just slapping some recipes together and waiting for the money to roll in. Not too long ago a couple of gurus suggested copying recipes off the web and putting 20-30 together into a cookbook. The idea is a list of recipe ingredients is not copyrightable. The instructions might be but all you had to do was change them some and reword them. This idea took off like wildfire and now Amazon is inundated with crappy little recipe books that are getting slammed by reviewers! Do you think reviews like the following are gonna sell many books for you?

★☆☆☆☆ **Wiki Links are NOT Writing!**, March 13, 2012
By saraf (Good Thunder, MN United States) - See all my reviews
Amazon Verified Purchase (What's this?)
This review is from: CHOCOLATE DESIRES (Kindle Edition)
Besides the fact this "author" starts the book with a plea for money, the "book" is horribly formatted and is merely a list of links to recipes on the web. To charge $8.99 for this is shameful...the "author" couldn't even be bothered to cut and paste the recipes? This person has several books on Amazon...and they are all the same. This book was offered free when I got it; if I had paid for it I'd be requesting a refund. As it is I will be deleting it from my archives.

★☆☆☆☆ **Low Quality Freshman Term Papers**, November 25, 2011
By Carson City, MI - See all my reviews
This review is from: Total And Unstoppable Confidence: 21 Experts Share Instant Ways To Develop Self-Esteem And Build Self-Confidence (Kindle Edition)
This is a collection of very poorly written articles which you will be embarrassed to even have on your Kindle. A Freshman English teacher would have a hard time getting through these term papers written by "experts". Please save your money and your time.

★☆☆☆☆ **Collection of Freshman Term Papers**, November 26, 2011
By Carson City, MI - See all my reviews
This review is from: The Healthy Vegetarian Diet Plan: 21 Experts Reveal The Health Benefits And Essential Vegetarian And Vegan Foods And Vitamins That Help You To Maintain Or Lose Weight (Kindle Edition)
This is not a collection of writings from "experts" but a collection of poorly written articles. Please don't waste your money.

In summary, this is a big, amateurish mess, and not worth your time or money. Whoever put it together should be ashamed. PASS!

If you are getting reviews like these on your books, chances are good that you deserve them for publishing total crap!!! You will not make any money like this so stop wasting your time. If you are going to get serious about Kindle publishing and making some money then you will have to put out quality books. Yes, it will take longer but one quality book is likely to make you more money than all your junk put together.

Some reviewers are so mad they are even tracking the recipes down on the web and putting their locations in their reviews. There have also been some angry threads in the Kindle Forum about this problem. Obviously this is not the way to publish cookbooks!

While we are talking about cutting and pasting stuff, I would like to touch on PLR. Amazon's main beef is that they were getting flooded with duplicate content. In some cases they had dozens of copies of the same thing up. Amazon made a wise decision to clean up their catalog to improve the customer experience. That being said, PLR does still have a place – if used right. I do sometimes use PLR material as a basis for my books and add to. I also don't see a problem using a few quality PLR articles to flesh out a book. A dozen PLR articles slapped together and called a book doesn't cut it! One thing that burns me up is the people slamming PLR as crap when they're still getting their stuff ghostwritten by the same people who used to churn out

PLR for them to sell. Its still the same crap – the only difference is now they only one using. There is a lot of very crappy PLR out there, but there is also some good stuff too if you are willing to look for and possibly pay a premium for. But even the good stuff needs some work so that its original. Whether you use PLR or not your book is only going to be as good as the materials you are working with. Garbage in – garbage out!

While we are on topic of copying and pasting stuff – you should know that images are also copyrighted. It is NOT ok to copy images off a website or Google images and use them in your own work. This is a good way to get sued! There are free stock images available out there. One of best places to start is http://www.sxc.hu/. If you are serious about your Kindle publishing, your best bet is to spend some money at a good stock photo site. Most images will only cost you a couple bucks and you will get higher quality images to use in your books. You might also wish to check out a great report I got off the Warrior Forum awhile back called **How To Find Totally FREE Graphics & Images Without Risking Your Business**. It's no longer available on WF but it is now available as a Kindle ebook. Besides all the great resources this book was a real eye-opener on how easy it is to track down illegal use of copyrighted images. So easy even you can do!

Public Domain Material

There has been some talk about using public domain material on Kindle and if its OK or not. Publishing public domain material on Kindle is fine if you follow **Amazon's rules**. They don't want a bunch of duplicate content listed so they require you to add to the material.

Selling content that is in the public domain is permissible through our program. We may request that you provide proof that your submitted material is actually in the public domain and may refuse public domain content already available through our Program or available through other retail sites.

In order to provide a better customer buying experience, our policy is to not publish undifferentiated versions of public domain titles where a free version is available in our store. We consider works to be differentiated when one or more of the following criteria are met:

• **(Translated)** - A unique translation
• **(Annotated)** - Contains annotations (unique, hand-crafted additional content including study guides, literary critiques, detailed biographies, or detailed historical context)
• **(Illustrated)** - Includes 10 or more unique illustrations relevant to the book

Books that meet this criteria must include (Translated), (Annotated), or (Illustrated) in the title field.

Notice the illustrated – you only have to include 10 or more unique illustrations and the book is considered differentiated! How easy is that? Public domain texts to get started with can be found in text format at many of the ebook download sites mentioned in this guide. Most works like this are low priced and Amazon only pays a 35% royalty; but if nicely done like these below can make you money.

I got lucky enough to find quite a few of these books on a free day. They are normally priced at only $0.99 so not real spendy anyway. Besides the nicely done covers that shows they related or part of series, the insides were nicely done with nice illustrations (most likely also public domain) and the formatting was good.

Formatting Issues

Kindle books need to look good on the inside as well as the cover. I have seen books with everything run together, bad formatting/grammar, centered text, words randomly broken between lines, and more. If your book looks sloppy, amateurish, or just unreadable people will be quick to refund and/or write bad reviews. Either way you end up not making any money.

Kindle formatting can be a real pain in the butt at times! I know from personal experience. But there are lots of guides and templates out there to make the process much easier. A professional looking book reflects highly on you the publisher. Don't worry too much if you don't get it perfect right away. I've noticed that even some of the big boys have formatting and grammatical errors in their books. Of course part of that could be not proofreading the stuff they get back from their $20 outsourcers? Taking some time to browse through books that interest you may also give you ideas for formatting your future books.

Some of the things I see that bug me and I frequently see reviewers complaining about:

- No clickable table of contents is one of the biggest complaints I see in bad reviews! If working in MS Word they are so easy to do. When formatting your book simply put your titles/subtitles in Heading 1, 2, or 3. Then go to References and pick Table of Contents and select your layout. That's it! Also, there is no need for page numbers in a Kindle book – so leave them out.
- Make your text readable. Paragraphs and some white space lot easier to read than text all run together. Unjustified or justified ok but don't center your text or right-align because its hard to read. Don't use oversized text, double-spaced. Not natural and

makes you look like you turning a little bit of nothing into a whole lot of fluff! If a reader needs larger text they can do enlarge with their Kindle.

- I personally like to see cover images inside the front of my Kindle books. It gives me a visual reference when I don't otherwise have one available. This not real big issue. What is a big issue is no cover at all! I won't download a book, even if its free, it it don't have any cover image.
- Reviewers frequently complain about everything being all run together – especially recipes. There is an easy solution for this in MS Word. Go to Insert and put in a page break before each section or recipe. This little tip alone will really clean up your book and make it look professionally laid out.
- Just how long should a book be? If you are gonna charge me book price then I expect a book. Don't pass off a glorified article as a book and charge me for a book. I'm likely to just feel ripped off! I don't mind articles or short books at all – as long as I know what I'm getting and they're priced accordingly.
- Don't forget about the **Look Inside** feature. This is typically about 10% of your book. Make it look good because many customers, including myself, will check this out to see if we want. If it looks like crap customers will quickly move on.
- A few thoughts on pen names. They're great! Use them for separate niches. I have seen a few names writing all over the board. This does make customers wonder. Also, the biggest customer base is American. If you have a name like Sri Vishwanath or Chinedum Azuh you might want to consider a pen name. Names like this make people wonder if your book is written in poor English and they're less apt to buy.

Mistakes and formatting errors bound to happen sometimes. One of the best things you can do to make sure your book looks the way you want it to is to actually buy yourself a copy. Do so when you got priced low at $0.99 or on a free promotional day. Actually open up the book in your Kindle and see if everything formatted right. If not make some changes and upload again. As long as same book you should be able to download again and check your revisions.

Print Editions

While browsing through books, I will pay attention to what other versions are offered. I will frequently look with suspicion upon books that are Kindle only. Reading through the Kindle Forum recently it seems other customers are doing the same. So much of the junk that is being churned out is Kindle only.

When I first started publishing, I simultaneously published to CreateSpace too. For those of you not familiar with, this is a print-on-demand publishing company also owned by Amazon. It's free to publish, other than ordering a proof copy will cost a few bucks. And formatting a book for CreateSpace is even easier than for Kindle! Their only downfall is that color photos inside your book prohibitively expensive.

My CreateSpace books have had some interesting results. On a couple of books I am actually selling as many print books as I am Kindle books! And my royalties are higher on the print books! I think that having a print edition available adds credibility to your Kindle book and helps sales of both formats. There isn't much more work involved either. I simply format one way for CreateSpace and then move to a Kindle template and do whatever tweaking I need to. CreateSpace also has a pretty good cover creator that I frequently use. To me this is basically getting 2 income streams for the price of one.

Reviews

I'm getting tired of everyone teaching to just go to Fiverr.com and buy reviews! So much so that I even recently requested a refund from someone saying to do this. Buying reviews directly against Amazon's TOS! The ONLY way you are allowed to compensate someone for a review is with a copy of your book. I suspect they are wise to this already. The worst thing about all those Kindle courses out there is that nobody is talking about legitimate ways to get reviews.

Conclusion

I hope you enjoyed this guide and that it has been informative and useful for you.

I also hope that if you are a Kindle publisher that you will use this guide as an aide to study what works and what doesn't on Amazon. Ultimately, the customer will be voting with their pocketbook. Make sure you are providing the quality books that keep them happy and it will be a win-win situation for everyone.

Now go find some good books! If you are like me your Kindle will be overflowing in no time! ☺

www.ingramcontent.com/pod-product-compliance
Lightning Source LLC
Chambersburg PA
CBHW041609180526
45159CB00002BC/790